7/03

D0569417

Staub, Frank J.
Alligators /
c1995.
33305013606904
GI   03/03/00

Alligators

written and photographed
by Frank Staub

 Lerner Publications Company • Minneapolis, Minnesota

SANTA CLARA COUNTY LIBRARY

3 3305 01360 6904

For Carlos, Nancy, Canyon, and Chase

The photographs in this book were taken in Louisiana at the Sabine and Rockefeller National Wildlife Refuges, Jungle Gardens on Avery Island, and Jean Lafitte National Historic Park. Additional photographs were taken at the Audubon Zoo and the Aquarium of the Americas, in New Orleans; Gatorland, in Orlando; and Everglades National Park.

Photograph on p. 25 reproduced through the courtesy of Rockefeller Wildlife Refuge.

Thanks to our series consultant, Sharyn Fenwick, elementary science/math specialist. Mrs. Fenwick was the winner of the National Science Teachers Association 1991 Distinguished Teaching Award. She also was the recipient of the Presidential Award for Excellence in Math and Science Teaching, representing the state of Minnesota at the elementary level in 1992. And special thanks to our young helper, Ben Liestman.

Special thanks to Ruth Elsey, Wildlife Biologist, for her assistance with the book.

The author would like to thank Ted Joanen, Louisiana Department of Wildlife and Fisheries; Les Hanna, Gatorland, in Orlando, Florida; Dr. C. Robert Shoop, University of Rhode Island; U.S. Fish and Wildlife Service; and the National Park Service for their assistance with this book.

Early Bird Nature Books were conceptualized by Ruth Berman and designed by Steve Foley. Series editor is Joelle Goldman.

Copyright © 1995 by Lerner Publications Company
All rights reserved. International copyright secured. No part of this book may be reproduced, stored in a retrieval system, or transmitted in any form or by any means, electronic, mechanical, photocopying, recording, or otherwise, without the prior written permission of Lerner Publications Company, except for the inclusion of brief quotations in an acknowledged review.

Library of Congress Cataloging-in-Publication Data

Staub, Frank J.
    Alligators / by Frank Staub
      p. cm. — (Early bird nature books)
    Includes index.
    ISBN 0-8225-3007-4
    1. Alligators–Juvenile literature. [1. Alligators.] I. Title. II. Series.
QL666.C925S73 1995
597.98–dc20   94-39112

Manufactured in the United States of America
2 3 4 5 6 7 – SP – 02 01 00 99 98 97

Contents

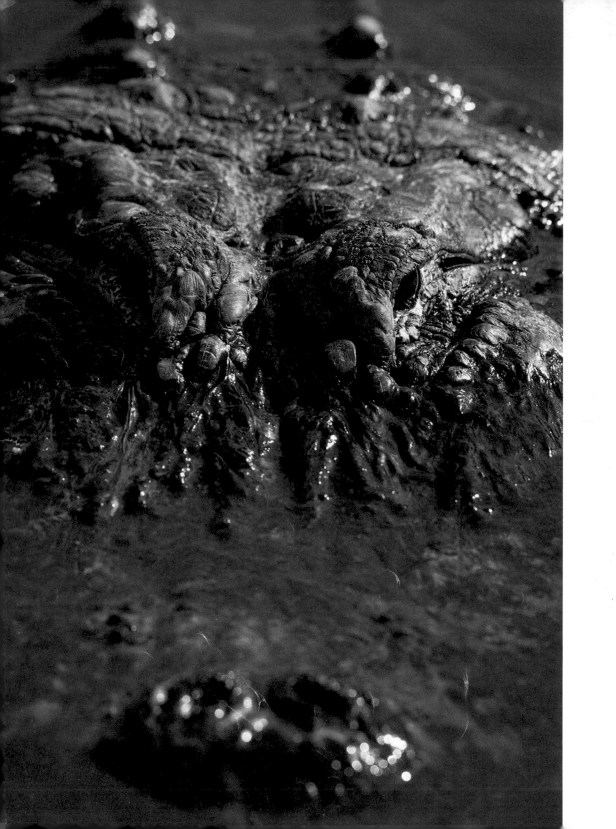

Alaska
(U.S.)

CANADA

N

UNITED STATES

The American alligator lives in the southeastern United States. The green areas show exactly where alligators live.

MEXICO

Be a Word Detective

Can you find these words as you read about the alligator's life? Be a detective and try to figure out what they mean. You can turn to the glossary on page 46 for help.

bask   ectotherm   predators
bellow   endotherm   prey
carnivores   'gator holes   reptile
crocodilians   hatchlings   wetlands

The scientific name of the American alligator is Alligator mississippiensis, *Where do you think alligators spend most of their time?*

A Monster in the Yard

Imagine a 10-foot-long monster walking into your yard. Its skin is dark and scaly. Its mouth is full of sharp teeth. Its jaws are strong enough to break your bones. Creatures like this really do walk into people's yards. But they aren't monsters. They're alligators.

American alligators spend most of their time floating in or lying next to water. They live in wetlands in the southeastern United States.

The only difference that can be seen between male and female alligators is that adult males grow bigger than the females.

Wetlands are land covered with water. Water may stay in a wetland all the time or just during part of the year. Rivers, lakes, swamps, and marshes are all wetlands. Alligators are usually found in freshwater wetlands. A freshwater wetland has little or no salt in it.

This bulrush marsh is a perfect wetland home for alligators.

Above: *Swamps are one kind of wetland.*

Right: *An alligator floats quietly among lily pads in Everglades National Park, Florida.*

People are filling in some wetlands with dirt so they can build houses on them.

Many wetlands are gone now. People have filled them in with dirt and rocks to make dry land. Some alligators living in those areas have nowhere else to go. So, every now and then, an alligator crawls into someone's yard. It's

Alligators can move quickly on land by walking on their toes. But they can't go far because their legs are so short.

probably looking for food in what used to be its home. Small dogs beware! An alligator can run fast when it stands on its toes and lifts its body off the ground. And a small dog would make a tasty meal for an alligator.

Chapter 2

Water snakes are related to alligators. Can you name the traits these two animals have in common?

Scaly Relatives

 The name "alligator" comes from the Spanish word for lizard—*el lagarto.* But alligators aren't lizards. Lizards don't grow nearly as big as alligators. Alligators are more like dinosaurs. Like dinosaurs and lizards, alligators are reptiles. All reptiles breathe air and have dry scaly skin. Snakes and turtles are reptiles too.

Alligators are part of a small group of animals called crocodilians (krah-keh-DIHL-ee-inz). All crocodilians have short legs and big, strong tails for swimming. The American crocodile is a crocodilian too. Crocodiles look a lot like alligators.

The American crocodile is a close relative of the alligator. The crocodile's scientific name is Crocodylus acutus.

It's easy to tell the difference between an alligator and a crocodile if you know what to look for. Crocodiles have thin, pointy snouts.

The alligator with its wide snout is on the left, and the pointy-nosed crocodile is on the right.

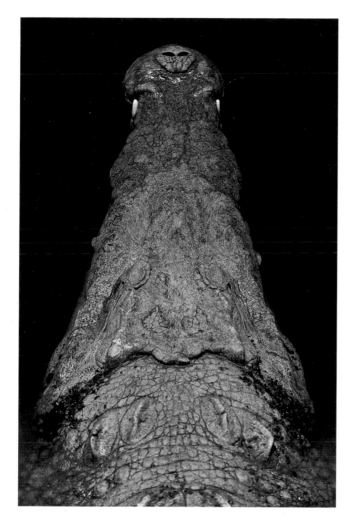

One way crocodiles differ from alligators is that crocodiles have two teeth that can be seen on the outside of their closed mouths.

Alligators have wide, rounded snouts. Most crocodiles can live in salty water. Most alligators live in freshwater. And when a crocodile closes its mouth, a tooth sticks up on each side of its lower jaw. In alligators, that tooth is hidden.

Chapter 3

Alligators lie in the sun to warm up. Do alligators spend time with other alligators?

Basking, Talking, and Fighting

Most of the time, alligators get along with each other just fine. They may bask together in groups along the shoreline. When an animal basks, it is usually lying in the sun.

Alligators, like this one basking in the sun, can live to be 75 years old.

Like all reptiles, alligators are cold-blooded. But their blood gets cold only when it's cold outside. A better name for a cold-blooded animal is ectotherm (EK-toh-therm). The body temperature of an ectotherm may change when the temperature outside its body changes.

When alligators become too warm, they may cool down in the water.

When alligators bask in the sun, their bodies warm up. If it is too hot outside, alligators find shade or go into the water.

People are warm-blooded animals. We are called endotherms (EN-doh-therms). The temperature inside our bodies stays the same no matter what the outside temperature is.

Alligators are usually quiet, but they can be noisy. Adult alligators make a loud roaring sound called a bellow. They bellow to get the attention of other alligators.

Alligators bellow for attention.

Alligators talk to each other with their bodies too. A male may arch his back, raising his head and tail up out of the water. Sometimes he slaps the water with his head. His body talk may be telling other alligators to come closer. But sometimes it tells them to stay away. He may also be making other alligators mad.

Alligators swim by moving their big, strong tails from side to side. They also use their tails in their body talk.

This alligator probably lost its foot in a fight with another alligator.

At times, alligators fight. They may just snap at each other, or they may actually bite. An alligator with a missing foot was probably hurt in a fight.

Chapter 4

Alligator eggs are about 3 inches long. How many eggs can there be in an alligator nest?

Good Mothers

Like all reptiles, alligators lay eggs. A reptile egg must stay dry. So the female alligator nests above the water. She builds her nest out of grass and mud. Alligator nests may be 3 feet high and 6 feet across. The female lays 20 to 50 eggs in a hole at the top of the nest. Then she covers up the hole. But she doesn't leave. A mother alligator stays close to her nest and guards it. She scares away raccoons, foxes, and other animals that like to eat alligator eggs. If another animal or a person comes too close, she will hiss. The hissing means, "Come any closer and I'll bite."

A mother alligator guarding her nest can be dangerous.

No matter how old she is, a female alligator is usually about 6 feet long before she builds a nest and lays her eggs.

Slowly, the grass in an alligator's nest rots. Rotting plants give off heat. Heat from the rotting plants helps the babies grow inside the eggs. If the temperature in the nest is very warm, most of the babies that hatch will be males. But if the nest is cool, there will be more females. Scientists are studying why this happens.

After about two months, little peeping sounds come from the nest. The babies are calling from inside the eggs. They may be calling to each other so that they all hatch at the same time. They are also calling to their mother, who uncovers the eggs. Sometimes she rolls the eggs around in her mouth to help the babies break free of their shells.

Baby alligators hatch about 65 days after the eggs were laid.

Baby alligators are called hatchlings right after they hatch. Hatchlings are about 8 inches long. At first, the hatchlings stay close to their mother. If a hatchling gets scared, it may make a high chirping sound. Then its mom comes to the rescue.

This hatchling is basking on its mother's back. When an alligator gets a little too hot, it may cool down by keeping its mouth open.

Alligators grow fastest when the weather is warm and they have plenty to eat. As they grow bigger, young alligators lose their yellow stripes.

Baby alligators grow fast—up to 1 foot a year during their first years of life. Male alligators may grow as long as a 12-foot rowboat. Females are a little shorter. The biggest alligator ever measured was over 19 feet long.

Chapter 5

This alligator is eating a fish. Can you name some of the other animals alligators like to eat?

Catching Meals

 Alligators are carnivores (KAHR-neh-vors). They eat animals not plants. An alligator can make a meal out of almost anything it can catch on land and in the water. Alligators are strong predators. Predators are animals that catch and eat other animals. The animals that a predator catches are its prey. The prey of young alligators are crayfish, insects, small fish, shrimp, and crabs. As alligators grow, they catch bigger and bigger prey. Adult alligators eat fish, birds, snakes, turtles, muskrats, and other alligators. A big alligator may even attack a deer that comes to the water for a drink.

Animals like this common moorhen would make a tasty meal for an alligator.

Alligators do most of their hunting at night. Darkness isn't a problem for them because they have a good sense of smell. Even during the day, alligators use their noses as well as their eyes to find food. Alligators also use their sense of hearing to catch their prey.

This unusual white alligator lives at the Audubon Zoo in New Orleans. All alligators can stay underwater because their eyes, nose, and ears are on top of their heads.

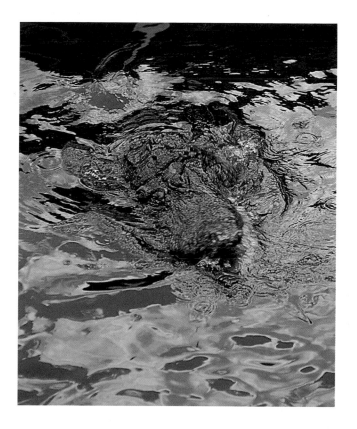

An alligator catches its meal.

Catching food in the water is easy for alligators. They can sneak up on their prey. An alligator swims quietly, without splashing. Its big tail moves back and forth, pushing the alligator forward. Most of the alligator's body is hidden under the water. Only its eyes and nose can be seen. A floating alligator may look like a log or a big leaf.

Sometimes alligators hunt by staying still in the water and waiting for an animal to swim by.

32

This alligator's inner eyelid is covering part of its eye.

The alligator sinks under water when it gets close to its prey. Clear inner eyelids protect its eyes. But the alligator can still see through these eyelids. The alligator attacks its prey from below or on the water's surface.

Alligator teeth are very strong. They are used for holding and tearing prey. Sometimes the teeth break. If one tooth is lost, a new one grows in to take its place. Alligators grow new teeth all through their lives.

Alligators have about 80 teeth. See if you can find places where this alligator has lost teeth.

Alligators don't chew their food, though. They swallow their prey whole. Our tongues help us swallow our food. But an alligator must stick its head straight up so its meal falls down its throat.

Alligators have to lift their heads up to swallow food.

Chapter 6

People have killed alligators for their skin and meat. Can you name some things that can be made out of alligator skin?

Living with Alligators

 A man once wrote that he saw so many alligators he could have walked across the water on their heads. Of course, he didn't try. That was 200 years ago. But from 1870 to 1970, 10 million wild alligators were killed for their meat and skins. An alligator's skin is worth a lot of money. It's tough, and it makes good shoes and handbags.

The U.S. government realized that too many alligators were being killed. So for a while, hunting alligators was against the law. Selling alligator skins used to be against the law too. Now in some areas there are a lot of alligators, and they can be hunted once again. But only a certain number of hunters are allowed to kill alligators.

No one knows exactly how many alligators are alive today, but there are many more alligators now than there were before 1970.

Chapter 7

Alligators help the wetlands by making 'gator holes. Do you know what a 'gator hole is?

The Helpful Monster

 People want to keep alligators around for many reasons. One reason is that they make 'gator holes. *'Gator* is a word that is short for alligator. A 'gator hole is a pond. It may be big or very small. An alligator uses its big body

A mother alligator has built her nest near a 'gator hole.

and tail to clear away plants and mud, making a low spot in the land. The low spot fills with water. If the rest of the wetland dries out, water usually stays in the 'gator hole.

'Gator holes help other wetland animals, like these egrets.

When there isn't much rain, birds, fish, frogs, and other animals come to 'gator holes to eat and drink. These animals make easy meals for the alligator.

Animals, like this swamp rabbit, come to 'gator holes and dens to eat and drink, but they have to watch out for hungry alligators.

Some alligators dig caves, or dens. The dens may be up to 30 feet deep. The opening to the den is usually under water. Air trapped at the end of the den lets the alligator breathe. During the winter, alligators spend a lot of time in their dens. Like 'gator holes, alligator dens hold water for fish and other animals during the dry season.

The nests alligators make also help wetland animals. Turtles, snakes, and some lizards lay eggs in alligator nests, sometimes while the alligators are still there. After the alligators leave, trees and other plants might grow in the nests. The trees give birds a place to make their

This mother alligator is guarding her nest. After her babies hatch, the nest could become dry land.

In zoos and on alligator farms, alligators are so well fed that they may not try to eat the other animals.

nests. As leaves and branches fall from the trees, the alligator nests turn into islands. Many animals live on these islands.

The world just wouldn't be the same without alligators. They are amazing animals. They may look like monsters. But alligators are creatures that other animals cannot live without.

On Sharing a Book

As you know, adults greatly influence a child's attitude toward reading. When a child sees you read, or when you share a book with a child, you're sending a message that reading is important. Show the child that reading a book together is important to you. Find a comfortable, quiet place. Turn off the television and limit other distractions, such as telephone calls.

Be prepared to start slowly. Take turns reading parts of this book. Stop and talk about what you're reading. Talk about the photographs. You may find that much of the shared time is spent discussing just a few pages. This discussion time is valuable for both of you, so don't move through the book too quickly. If the child begins to lose interest, stop reading. Continue sharing the book at another time. When you do pick up the book again, be sure to revisit the parts you have already read. Most importantly, enjoy the book!

Be a Vocabulary Detective

You will find a word list on page 5. Words selected for this list are important to the understanding of the topic of this book. Encourage the child to be a word detective and search for the words as you read the book together. Talk about what the words mean and how they are used in the sentence. Do any of these words have more than one meaning? You will find these words defined in a glossary on page 46.

What about Questions?

Use questions to make sure the child understands the information in this book. Here are some suggestions:

What did this paragraph tell us? What does this picture show? What do you think we'll learn about next? What would you need to live where alligators live? Could alligators live in your backyard? Why/Why not? What do you think it's like living in wetlands? What do you think it's like being an alligator? What would happen if there were no alligators? What is your favorite part of the book? Why?

If the child has questions, don't hesitate to respond with questions of your own, such as: What do *you* think? Why? What is it that you don't know? If the child can't remember certain facts, turn to the index.

Introducing the Index

The index is an important learning tool. It helps readers get information quickly without searching throughout the whole book. Turn to the index on page 47. Choose an entry, such as *nests,* and ask the child to use the index to find out what alligators use to make their nests. Repeat this exercise with as many entries as you like. Ask the child to point out the differences between an index and a glossary. (The index helps readers find information quickly, while the glossary tells readers what words mean.)

All the World in Metric!

Although our monetary system is in metric units (based on multiples of 10), the United States is one of the few countries in the world that does not use the metric system of measurement. Here are some conversion activities you and the child can do using a calculator:

WHEN YOU KNOW:	MULTIPLY BY:	TO FIND:
miles	1.609	kilometers
feet	0.3048	meters
inches	2.54	centimeters
gallons	3.787	liters
tons	0.907	metric tons
pounds	0.454	kilograms

Activities

Imagine being an alligator. Move like an alligator would move on land. How does an alligator run? Act out how an alligator eats. How does an alligator stay warm?

Body language is a big part of how alligators communicate. Try to "talk" to the rest of your family by using body language.

Visit a zoo to see alligators. See how many different reptiles you can find.

Make a clay model of an alligator. Now tell a story about your clay alligator using information you've learned in this book.

Glossary

bask—to lie in warmth

bellow—to make a loud, deep sound like a roar

carnivores (KAHR-neh-vors)—animals who eat flesh or meat

crocodilians (krah-keh-DIHL-ee-inz)—animals including alligators, crocodiles, caimans, and gavials who are scientifically grouped together

ectotherm (EK-toh-therm)—a cold-blooded animal

endotherm (EN-doh-therm)—a warm-blooded animal

'gator holes—ponds made by alligators

hatchlings—baby animals who have just hatched from eggs

predators—animals who hunt other animals for food

prey—an animal who is hunted by another animal for food

reptile—a cold-blooded animal who crawls on short legs or moves on its belly

wetlands—land areas with a lot of moisture

Index

Pages listed in **bold** type refer to photographs.

About the Author

Frank Staub is a former high school science teacher now working as a freelance writer and photographer. He specializes in nature, people, and adventure sports, which allows him to travel to and study the places and events that intrigue him the most. He has a bachelor of science degree in biology and a master of science degree in zoology. His writing and photography have appeared in numerous books, magazines, and educational materials. Mr. Staub is the writer and photographer for Lerner's Early Bird Nature Books titles *Mountain Goats* and *Sea Turtles,* and is the photographer for *Giant Sequoia Trees.* He is also the writer and photographer for Carolrhoda's Earth Watch titles *America's Prairies, Yellowstone's Cycle of Fire,* and *America's Wetlands.* When he's not working, he enjoys bicycling, climbing mountains, sea kayaking, and skin diving.